CW01498901

Index

1st inning - Introduction
Holy Cow! Is that a rule?

A journey through the ever changing rules of baseball

Baseball was different when the American people embraced it almost two centuries ago. There were no stadiums or stands with seats. There were no fences or foul poles, no dugouts or bull pens. Just an open field, four bases and a spot designated as the Pitcher's position. Those who occupied that spot were called "Servers" at the time and their job was to accommodate the "Batsman" who occupied a position of his own. The Server's job was to serve the man with the lumber rather than conquer him, even if they were on opposing missions. The game was about hitting and scoring runs which were called "aces" and the first team to score 21 aces was the winner.

Pitchers often made their own balls and batters whittled bats until they became functional. Outs could be recorded by catching a batted ball on the fly as well as on one bounce. And if the Umpire wasn't sure if a good catch was made, he simply asked the spectators. Today we call them fans but back then they were known as "cranks" who sometimes got involved in the game play. By rule at the time, a ball in play that got loose among the bystanders was a live ball that could be kicked around by the cranks while base runners scampered around the bases.

The founders of early baseball in America saw the need for rules and established a constitution for the teams and the people involved as well as rules of the game and the intent was that of seriousness. A constitution rule stated that a player who became indifferent or careless in his play could result in the club refusing to pay his salary. Of a similar nature a playing rule said that a runner returning to his base after a foul ball should "return on the run and not at a walk."

Many old rules did not pass the test of time and many others survived with some tweaking. And today of course, the Lords of Baseball continue to tweak the rules just as they have done for almost two hundred years,

Perhaps it's time to take a trip through the ever changing rules of baseball.

Holy Cow! – One bounce outs.

From the beginning, in 1845 a batter was out if the ball he hit was caught on one bounce or on the fly. That applied to balls hit both fair or foul. One bounce outs came to an end in 1865 for fair balls, but continued until 1883 for foul balls.

2nd inning - Old rules and old words

Old rules

1 - Ump fining Pitchers

1884 - RULE 62. *If the Pitcher causes the ball to strike the Batsman*, and the Umpire be satisfied that he does it intentionally, he shall fine the pitcher therefore in a sum not less than Ten Dollars, nor more than Fifty Dollars.

2 - Police assistance

1887 - Rule 19. Every club shall furnish sufficient police force upon its own grounds to preserve order, and in the event of a crowd entering the field during the progress of a game, and interfering with the play in any manner, the Visiting Club may refuse to play further until the field be cleared. If the ground be not cleared within fifteen minutes thereafter, the Visiting Club may claim, and shall be entitled to, the game by a score of nine runs to none (no matter what number of innings have been played).

3 - Train schedule

1895 - Sec. 52. On any day when either club is required to leave a city to, or in order to reach another city, where it is scheduled to play its next game, the home club shall be compelled upon proper notice by the visiting club to begin the game three hours anil a half before the time of the departure of the last train by means of which either club can reach the next scheduled point in time. And either club may leave the field at any time within one hour of said train time without forfeiting any rights or privileges, provided five innings have been played, and the Umpire shall be the sole judge of the time.

Old words

1 - Foul strike

A "Foul Strike" is a ball batted by the batsman when either or both of his feet are upon the ground outside the lines of the box.

1877 rules - Rule 5, sections 8 and 9

The Batsman must stand within the lines of his position. Should he step outside the lines when he strikes the ball, the Umpire shall call "foul strike" and "out."

2 - Foul balk

1877 - Rule 4, section 3 - Should the Pitcher deliver the ball by an overhand motion, a "foul balk" shall be called.
1877 - Rule 4, section 4 - When a "foul balk" is called, the Umpire shall warn the Pitcher. If there are 3 foul balks in one inning the Umpire shall declare a forfeit.

3 - Blocked balls

Holy Cow! - Blocked balls.
In the late 1800's a "blocked ball" was defined as a batted or thrown ball that is stopped or handled by any person not engaged in the game. In other words, spectators. And in such cases any base runners were allowed to freely scamper around the bases until the ball was returned to the Pitcher. Spectators often took the liberty to keep the ball or

kick it away if it favored the team they were rooting for. It took until 1940 to get this one right.

1900 – Rule 35. — Block Balls.

Section 1. A Block is a batted or thrown ball that is touched, stopped or handled by any person not engaged in the game.

Section. 2. Whenever a block occurs the umpire shall declare it, and the base-runners may run the bases without being put out until the ball has been returned to and held by the pitcher standing in his position.

Section. 3. In the case of a block, if the person not engaged in the game should retain possession of the ball, or throw or kick it beyond the reach of the fielders, the umpire should call "Time" and require each base-runner to stop at the last base touched by him until the ball be returned to the pitcher standing in his position and the umpire shall have called " Play."

1934 - Rule 33, sections 2 and 3

Base runners are free to advance on a blocked ball but the Umpire can call "time" if the fan keeps the ball or kicks it or throws it beyond the reach of a fielder.

1940 - Rule 33

Balls handled by spectators are "dead balls."

1942 - Rule 33 –Base runner NOT free to advance when ball is touched by a spectator

4 - Fair and unfair balls

Fair (strikes) and unfair (balls) pitches entered the rule books when pitchers began ignoring the "over the center of home base" guideline. Rather they would intentionally throw the pitches outside the zone hoping the batters would tire of waiting for the perfect pitch and swing at one that was less likely to be hit with authority.

1873 – First definition of fair and unfair balls although fair balls were indicated in 1864.

Fair Balls – "All balls delivered to the bat which are sent in over the Home Plate and "high" or "low" as the batsman calls for and which are not delivered by an overhand throw or by a round arm delivery as in Cricket."

Unfair Balls - All balls delivered by the pitcher, striking the ground before reaching the line of the home base, or pitched over the head of the batsman, or pitched to the side opposite to that which the batsman strikes from, shall be considered unfair balls.

1877 - Rule 4, section 7 - Balls delivered by the Pitcher which are not sent in over Home base and at the height called for by the Batsman shall be considered "unfair balls." When 3 unfair balls have been called, the Striker shall take first base.

5 - Fairly and unfairly delivered balls, word changes

1900 – Rule 30. — A Fairly Delivered Ball.

A Fairly Delivered Ball to the bat is a ball pitched or thrown to the bat by the pitcher while standing in his position and facing the batsman, the ball so delivered to pass over any portion of the home base not lower than the batsman's knee nor higher than his shoulder.

1900 - Rule 31. — An Unfairly Delivered Ball.

An Unfairly Delivered Ball is a ball delivered by the pitcher, as in Rule 30, except that the ball does not pass over any portion of the home base, or does pass over the home base, above the batsman's shoulder or below the line of his knee.

1934 rules - Rule 28 and 29 - <u>Fairly and unfairly delivered balls</u>
A fairly delivered ball is one pitched within the strike zone, an unfairly delivered ball is outside the strike zone.

5 - Dead balls and Illegal balls

Dead Ball – "Delivered by the Pitcher that touches the Batsman's bat without being struck at, or any part of the Umpire's person without first passing the Catcher."

1884 – Illegal Ball – "Sent in by the Pitcher after he has raised his foot from the rear line of the box or after taking more than one step in his delivery, or after stepping outside the line of his position or after failing to resume his standing position before delivering the ball after making a feint to throw to a base."
Penalty – Batsman given his base.

3rd inning - The Playing Field

1 - Pitcher's position and the mound

This is an area that baseball fiddled with a lot in the early years. In1857 it was an Iron plate 4 yards long. The distance to home was 15 yards. In 1864 the Pitchers position consisted of 2 lines 4 yards long and 1 yard deep. Before the decade ended the dimensions had changed three more times so that in 1869 those 2 lines were two yards long and two yards apart. A nice little rectangle that the server did his thing from.

It took another fifteen years before the planners played around again with the domain of the Pitcher. This time, in 1884 the lines were 6 feet long and 4 feet apart. Three years later they decided that 6 feet was too long so they shortened the lines to 5 ½ feet. And there it stayed until the magical year of 1893 when the game would change forever.

For the 1893 season the rectangles had disappeared, to be replaced by a rubber plate 12 inches long and 4 inches deep. It would remain so for the rest of time, to the current day at least. The more dramatic changes that year involving the Pitcher's area were twofold. First the distance from that rubber plate was set at 60 feet, 6 inches (history is not sure how that precise number came up) which it remains to this day. The second major change was the creation of a Pitcher's mound. Until then the hurlers threw from flat ground, level with the rest of the playing field. Now the Pitcher would be throwing the ball at a downward angle which would turn the tide to advantage Pitcher after so many years of being a foil for the batter.

There were no immediate regulations regarding the "mound" just the OK to create one so groundskeepers did whatever the ownership told them to do, Some changed the height according to the skills of the teams they would be playing, most tried to determine the most efficient height for their Pitchers. Finally in 1905 the league mandated that the mound could not be higher than 15 inches above the rest of the field. Then it took another lengthy period of time until 1950 when it was required that all mounds be had to be 15 inches high.

That lasted until 1969 when the height of all mounds was lowered to 10 inches.

Rule 1.04 in 1969 - lowered the height of the pitcher's mound from 15 to 10 inches and specified the slope: "The infield shall be graded so that the base lines and home plate are level. The pitcher's plate shall be ten inches above the level of home plate. The degree of slope from a point 6 inches in front of the pitcher's plate to a point 6 feet toward home plate shall be 1 inch to 1 foot, and such degree shall be uniform."

2 - Pitching distance

The distance from the Pitcher's position to home base, or home plate changed a bit also over the years. In 1864 it was defined as 15 paces. In 1859 the wording changed to 15 yards which was probably a more accurate description of 15 paces. Then in 1871 the distance was listed as 45 feet which was just a change of wording.

In 1881 they moved it back a bit to 50 feet and in 1893 to 60 feet, 6 inches where it remains to the present day.

3 - Fences

Holy Cow! – Over the Fence Doubles
Before there were outfield fences a batter could launch a long drive beyond the reach of fielders and circle the bases for a home run. When fences became a reality, rules in the late 1800's stated

that a fence had to be at least 210 feet away for a batted ball clearing it to be a home run, otherwise it was a double. Later that distance changed to 235 feet and in 1926, 250 feet.

1934 - Rule 41, section 2 - Ground rule double if batted ball goes over a fence on the fly if the fence is less than 250 feet from home plate.

Oddly enough that rule remains in the current rule book (2025 rule 5.05a(5) even though the current rules also require new fields to have a minimum distance to any fence be 325 feet. Also strange is the fact that the rules, until 1931 said that a batted ball bouncing into the stands was a home run.

4 - On deck circle

There are no rules about the on deck circle other than in the appendix for field layout, there are two 5 foot diameter circles called the "next batter's box." Contrary to what is commonly believed, a player is not required to wait in the on deck circle for his turn at bat. It is just one of baseball's customs that might become a rule if batter's started waiting in closer to the action or maybe directly behind the catcher to see what the pitcher had. But they don't, they stay in that area where the circle is dutifully chalked before each game while they wait for their turn at bat.

4th inning - Equipment

1 – Bats

By the early 1860's there were several different types of bats in use. Bats were long and short, thin and thick and many a batter whittled their own that might not fit in any particular pattern. For the most part however, bats in the early days tended to be larger and heavier than future generations.

Eventually though, bat sizes became subject to the rules like other aspects of the game.

In 1857 the rules stated that a bat could be any length and not more than 2 ½ inches diameter at its thickest part. In 1868 the length was limited to 42 inches maximum.

In 1876 the rules dictated that the bat must be round and made of wood

There has never been a minimum length

Holy Cow! – flat bats

That's right, for a brief period in the early days, from1885 until 1892, one side of the bat could be flat.

1885 - Rule 14(2) - The bat must be round, except that a portion of the surface may be flat on one side, must not exceed two and one-half inches in diameter in the thickest part of the bat, and must not exceed forty-two inches in length

1893 – Rule 13 - flat bats prohibited, not specifically but by the deletion of the wording stating it could have a flat side.

Private bats

The one year rule about private bats
1873 - The striker shall be privileged to use his own private bat exclusively, and no other player of the contesting nines shall have any claim to the use of such, except by consent of its owner.

[No player of the contesting nine has the right to use a player's private bat, or even a bat belonging to the opposing nine, without the consent of the owner or the opposing party.]

2 - Balls

In the beginning Pitchers usually made their own baseballs and they were similar to those that would soon be regulated by size and weight.

In 1854 the rules required baseballs to weigh between 5 ½ and 6 ounces. Over the next decade that would vary slightly but eventually settle at 5 to 5 ¼ ounces with a circumference of 9 to 9 1.4 inches.

Winner gets the ball

1877 - Rule 1, section 1 - The ball or balls should be furnished by the home club and shall become the property of the winning club.

1934 - Rule 14, section 5 - Winning team keeps last ball in play.

As late as 1946 the rules still had the last ball used in a game going to the winner.

Lost balls

1877 - Rule 1, section 4 - Should the ball be lost during a game, the Umpire shall, at the expiration of five minutes, call for a new ball.

Balls must have been hard to come by if they actually had a rule for how long they had to look for a lost ball before giving up and using a new one.

Holy Cow! – Cowhide balls
Organized baseball dictated that balls should be covered by leather from the onset of official rules. And they were usually covered by horsehide, until 1972 when the rules stated that baseballs could be covered by cowhide as well. A rule most likely dictated by a shortage of horses. In time one can guess that a plastic like substance will become common.

3 - Gloves

1900 - SEC. 2. The catcher and first baseman are permitted to wear a glove or mitts of any size, shape or weight. All other players are restricted to the use of a glove or not weighing not over ten ounces, and measuring in circumference, around the palm of the hand, not over fourteen inches

There are NO rules requiring fielders to wear gloves

5th inning - People

1 - The Managers and Captains

Choice of innings

Holy Cow! – Who bats first?
The rule books call it "choice of innings" and for the first hundred years of organized baseball it was decided by the team Captains. Simply put, they would decide which team bats in the top of the innings and which in the bottom. Before managers existed, team Captains ran the show, assigning fielding positions, making out the line-up, and choosing innings. Later the home team Captain made the choice. This prevailed as late as 1950. In 1951 Rule 4.02 stated that the home team will take defensive positions to start the game, and the first batter for the visiting team will take his position in the batter's box. That had been the custom for many years, it just took a century to put it in writing.

1934 Rule 26 - The Manager or Captain of the home team has the choice of innings

Choice of innings end

1951 Rule 4.02 - Players from home team take defensive positions first.

The Manager and Line-up cards

Holy Cow! – the line-up cards,

For a lot of years the rules have stated that the home team manager must present his line-up card first to the umpire at the start of a game. Then the visiting team manager must present his line-up card.

Does this really matter and warrant a rule?

1951 Rule 4.01 - The home team Manager must give line-up card to the Umpire **First**

This rule is still in effect in 2025

2 - The Umpire

Celebrity Umps

Back in 1860 people other than players wanted to be involved in the game. Lacking the skill to play, being an umpire had appeal, such that they had to pass a rule aimed at deterring the so called "ceremonial umpires."

1860 rule, Sec. 34. - No person shall be permitted to act as umpire or scorer in any match, unless he shall be a member of a Base-Ball Club governed by these rules. Prohibits *"ceremonial"* umpires, such as local politicians or other prominent citizens who may have little knowledge of the game. For our purposes, it is important that umpires be very familiar with the specific year's rules and playing customs.

Spectator Umps

Holy Cow! – Fans make the call
Way back in 1876 when most baseball games had only one umpire it was difficult to get all the necessary calls right. There were no foul lines drawn on the field so the rules allowed the umpire

to ask spectators if a batted ball had been fair or foul if his view had been obscured. The umpire could also solicit help from the crowd about whether a fielder had indeed made a catch of a batted ball. That all ended in 1882 but for a brief time, everyone had an opinion and sometimes it affected a play on the field.

1877 Rule 7, section 5 - Should the Umpire be unable to see whether a catch has been fairly made or not, he shall be at liberty to appeal to the bystanders and render his decision according to the fairest testimony at command.

Panic situation

Holy Cow! – A Panic Situation.
Sometime around 1950 this odd rule appeared in the books. "In the case of fire, panic or storm, the Umpire does not have to wait until the Pitcher has the ball on the mound to call a Time-Out.

One can envision a hurricane and a very patient Umpire waiting for the Pitcher to be in position and with the ball in his hand, before calling time out.

Creating rules

Holy Cow! – Umpire can make up rules if not in the rule book

1970 - Rule 9.00 (c) - Each Umpire has authority to rule on any point not specifically covered in these rules.
This rule is still in the 2025 rule book

Lone Ump

1970 - Rule 9.03 - If there is only one Umpire he can rule from any place on the field. Usually behind the Catcher but if there are men on base, he may stand behind the Pitcher.
This rule is still in the 2025 rule book

6th inning - The game

1 - Pitching

The rules were detailed and precise on just how a Pitcher could go about his business

Pitchers motion

1857 - The ball must be pitched, not jerked nor thrown to the bat; and whenever the pitcher draws back his hand, or moves with the apparent purpose or pretension to deliver the ball, he shall so deliver it, and he must have neither foot in advance of the front line or off the ground at the time of delivering the ball; and if he fails in either of these particulars, then it shall be declared a baulk.

* The pitcher makes a baulk when he either jerks a ball to the bat, has either foot in advance of the line of his position, or off the ground at the time of delivering the ball, or moves with the apparent purpose of pitching, without delivering the ball The sentence "time of delivering the ball" has been interpreted by the Committee on Rules and Regulations of the National Association to mean, the period when the last movement of the arm is made in delivering the ball; and consequently if either foot of the pitcher be off the ground when this movement is made-it being nearly simultaneous with the ball's leaving the hand of the pitcher-umpires must declare a baulk without being appealed to.

Pitcher limitations

1864 – "The pitcher must stand between the lines (4 yards by 1 yard) and deliver the ball as near as possible over the Home Base".

1873 – "The Pitcher must deliver the ball while within the lines of the Pitcher's position and he must remain within the lines until the ball has left his hand. He shall not make any motion to deliver the ball while outside the lines of the Pitcher's position."

1887 – "The Pitcher shall take his position facing the Batsman with both feet squarely on the ground, the right foot on the rear line of the box. His left foot in advance of the right and to the left of an imaginary line from his right foot to the center of Home Base. He shall not raise his foot unless in the act of delivering the ball, nor make more than one step in such delivery. He shall hold the ball, before delivery, fairly in front of his body and in sight of the Umpire. When the Pitcher feigns to throw the ball to a base, he must resume the above position and pause momentarily before delivering the ball."

(Reversed for a left handed Pitcher)

The Pitch Clock

Today's rules mandate that the Pitcher must make his pitch within 15 seconds. The Batter also has to be in the batter's box within 8 seconds. This rule has gotten a lot of attention in the last few years with "pitch violations" a common occurrence. In reality, the pitch clock rule has been around for a long time, and mostly ignored.

1901 Rule - "The umpire shall call a ball on the pitcher each time he delays the game by failing to deliver the ball to the batsman for a longer period than 20 seconds."

1934 Rule 30, section 2 – delaying the game
The Umpire shall call a ball on the Pitcher each time he delays the game by failing to deliver the ball to the batsman for a longer period than 20 seconds.

The rule has changed over the years. It was 20 seconds in the 1990's, flipped between 12 and 20 seconds after the turn of the century.

In 2006, by which time games were a full hour longer, on average, than they had been in 1901—MLB made an amendment: "When the bases are unoccupied, the pitcher shall deliver the ball to the batter within 12 seconds after he receives the ball." This year's 15-second ceiling with the bases empty is less strict than that. In other words, the rule book has called for a pitch clock for most of baseball's history. The only difference this season is that MLB is belatedly heeding that call in a concerted fashion.

And even today in 2025 the rules in print differ from the rules in practice.

2025 Rule 5.07(c) - When the bases are unoccupied, the pitcher shall deliver the ball to the batter within 12 seconds after he receives the ball. Each time the pitcher delays the game by violating this rule, the umpire shall call "Ball."
The 12-second timing starts when the pitcher is in possession of the ball and the batter is in the box, alert to the pitcher. The timing stops when the pitcher releases the ball.

Contrary to popular belief there is NO rule about 18 seconds with runners on base.

There is also NO rule about the Pitcher and Batter making eye contact, only a rule stating that the Pitcher must be facing the batter when he delivers the ball.

At any rate, the pitch clock rule is not new, it's been around for a very long time, they just dusted off the cobwebs in recent years.

Pitcher Illegal Action

2025 - 6.02 Pitcher Illegal Action

Rule 6.02(b) Comment: A ball which slips out of a pitcher's hand and crosses the foul line shall be called a ball; otherwise it will be called no pitch. This would be a balk with men on base

2 – Hitting

Batter Position and limitations

1857 – "The Striker must stand on a line drawn through the center of Home base, the line not exceeding 3 feet either side."

1868 – "The Striker, when about to strike the ball must stand astride a line drawn through the center of Home Base, and he must not take any backward step when striking the ball. The penalty for failing to do so is a called ball."

1873 – "The Striker, when in the act of striking at the ball, must stand astride the line and distant not less than one foot from the base. Only one foot must be forward or backward of the Home Base line. The penalty for failing to do so is a foul strike. If he hits the ball during this foul strike call and it is caught he is out."

Refusing to strike

Should the striker refuse to strike at balls pitched over the home base, and within the specified reach of the bat, the umpire shall call "one strike," and if the striker persists in such action, two and three strikes. When three strikes are called, and the ball be caught, either before touching the ground or upon the first bound, the striker shall be declared out, provided the balls struck at are not those on which balls or balks have been called. If three balls are struck at and missed, and the last one is not caught, either flying or upon the first bound, the striker (or the player running for him) must attempt to make his run, and in such cases he can be put out on the bases in the same manner as if he had struck a fair ball. No strike shall be called upon the first ball delivered except the ball be struck at, and neither shall any strike be called when the ball is struck at for the purpose of willfully striking out.

Calling pitch location

Holy Cow! – The Batsman can call his pitches.
From 1864 to 1886 the Batsman could inform the Umpire that he wanted all pitches in that at bat, either high or low. The Ump would inform the Pitcher who was then obligated to toss his pitches low (knees to waist) or high (waist to shoulders) and to throw it over the plate.

Batter Calling for balls 1873

The striker shall be privileged to call for either a high or a low ball, in which case the pitcher must deliver the ball to the bat as required. The ball shall be considered a high ball if pitched between the height of the waist and the shoulder of the striker; and it shall be considered a low ball if pitched between the height of the waist and one foot from the ground.

Balls not called for
Should the striker fail to call for either a "high" or "low" ball, in such case no ball shall be called which is delivered over the home base and within the range of shoulder high, and one foot from the ground; provided, also, that the balls so delivered shall not include any balls described in rule 2, section 4th, as "unfair balls.

1877 Rule 5, section 5 - The Batter must call for either a "high ball," a "low ball," or a "fair ball." The Umpire shall notify the Pitcher.
This change allowed the batter to ask for a "fair ball" which meant just over the plate, not necessarily high or low.

3 - The Designated Hitter

Interesting Designated Hitter rules

The Pitcher can pinch hit or pinch run for the Designated Hitter, and only for the DH.

The Designated Hitter is not allowed to sit in the Bullpen unless he serves as a Bullpen Catcher.

If a defensive player replaces the Pitcher, the Designated Hitter rule is terminated

Then there's these confusing words

2025 – Rule 5.11 Designated Hitter Rule

(a) The Designated Hitter Rule provides as follows:

(1) A hitter may be designated to bat for the starting pitcher and all subsequent pitchers in any game without otherwise affecting the status of the pitcher(s) in the game. A Designated Hitter for the pitcher, if any, must be selected prior to the game and must be included in the lineup cards presented to the umpire-in-chief. If a manager lists 10 players in his team's lineup card, but fails to indicate one as the Designated Hitter, and an umpire or either manager (or designee of either manager who presents his team's lineup card) notices the error before the umpire-in-chief calls "Play" to start the game, the umpire-in-chief shall direct the manager who had made the omission to designate which of the nine players,

2025 - Rule 5.11 (b)

It is not mandatory that a Club designate a hitter for the pitcher. However, in the event the starting pitcher will bat for himself, the player will be considered two separate people for purposes of Rule 5.11(a). In such cases, the manager should list 10 players on his team's lineup card, and this player should be named twice – once as the starting pitcher and once as the Designated Hitter. Thus, if the starting pitcher is replaced, he can continue as the Designated Hitter (but can no longer pitch in the game), and if the Designated Hitter is replaced, he can continue as the pitcher (but can no longer hit for himself). If the player is simultaneously replaced both as a starting pitcher and Designated Hitter, he cannot be replaced by another two-way player filling both roles as separate people (this can be done only once on the initial lineup card by identifying that the starting pitcher will bat for himself)Notwithstanding anything to the contrary in Rule 5.11(a) above, if that pitcher bats or runs as Designated Hitter, such move will not terminate the Designated Hitter role for that Club; neither will the role be terminated in the event that Designated Hitter assumes the role of pitcher on defense.

However, if that player is switched from the mound or Designated Hitter role to a position on defense other than the Pitcher, such move will terminate the Designated Hitter for that club for the remainder of the game.

4 - Strikes and strikeouts

1845 – 3 swings and misses are a strikeout. There were no called strikes at that time. Until 1858 a batter had to swing and miss 3 soft underhand tosses to strike out. An unlikely event.

1858 – "Should a Striker stand at the bat without striking at good balls repeatedly pitched to him, for the purpose of delaying the game, or giving advantage to a player, the Umpire, after warning him shall call one strike. And, if he persists in such action, two and three strikes."

That rule was expanded 10 years later.

1868 – Should a striker stand at the bat without striking at fair balls for the apparent purpose of delaying the game, or of giving advantage to a player, the umpire, after warning him, shall call one strike, and if he persists in such action, two and three strikes. When three strikes are called, and the ball be caught, either before touching the ground or upon the first bound, the striker shall be declared out, provided the balls struck at are not those on which balls or balks have been called, or not those struck at for the purpose of willingly striking out. If three balls are struck at and missed, and the last one is not caught, either flying or upon the first bound, the striker must attempt to make his run, and he can be put out on the bases in the same manner as if he had struck a fair ball. *(This last section has been combined from several rules.)*

1877 Rule 5, section 7 - Should the Striker fail to strike at the ball he calls for, or should he strike at and fail to hit the ball, the Umpire shall call a "strike." After 2 strikes if the Batsman does not strike at the next "good ball" the Umpire shall warn him by calling "fair ball." If he then fails to strike at or strike at and hit the next "good ball," three strikes are called and the Batsman must run to first base as if he had hit a fair ball, and the Catcher is required to throw him out the same as any infielder.

1880 – Warning no longer needed.

1887 – Four strikes were a strikeout for that year only

5 - The strike zone

1876 – Batters still called for pitch location, High ball – waist to shoulders
Low ball waist to one foot off the ground
1877 – Waist changed to "belt." Lower limit became the knee.
1887 – Batters no longer can call pitch location. Strike zone is shoulders to the knees.
1950 – Arm pits to top of knees

1963 Rule - The Strike Zone is that space over home plate which is between the top of the batter's shoulders and his knees when he assumes his natural stance. The umpire shall determine the Strike Zone according to the batter's usual stance when he swings at the pitch.

1969 - The Strike Zone is that space over home plate which is between the batter's armpits and the top of his knees when he assumes a natural stance. The umpire shall determine the Strike Zone according to the batter's usual stance when he swings at a pitch.

1988 - The Strike Zone is that area over home plate, the upper limit of which is a horizontal line at the midpoint between the top of the shoulders and the tip of the uniform pants, and the lower level is a line at the top of the knees. The Strike Zone shall be determined from the batter's stance as the batter is prepared to swing at a pitch ball.

1996 - The Strike Zone is expanded on the lower end, moving from the top of the knees to the bottom of the knees (bottom has been identified as the hollow beneath the kneecap).

6 - Balls and walks

3 Ball Walks

1864 – "Should the Pitcher repeatedly fail to deliver to the Striker fair balls, for the apparent purpose of delaying the game, or for any other cause, the Umpire, after warning him shall call one ball. And, if the Pitcher persists in such action, two and three balls. When three balls have been called the Striker shall be entitled to First Base,"

1866 – Should the pitcher repeatedly fail to deliver to the striker fair balls, for the apparent purpose of delaying the game, or for any other cause, the umpire, after warning him, shall call one ball, and if the pitcher persists in such action, two and three balls; when three balls shall have been called, the striker shall be entitled to the first base; and should any base be occupied at that time, each player occupying them shall be entitled to one base without being put out. In warning the pitcher before calling balls on him, all that is necessary is to call "ball to the bat;" and if two balls are pitched unfairly after such warning, "one ball" should be called, and if one unfair ball be delivered after that call, then "two" and "three" balls should be promptly called. A pitcher "repeatedly" fails if he fails twice in succession; and he "persists" in his unfair delivery if he pitch one ball after the first penalty has been imposed. In the first innings of a game, a little more latitude is allowable, but afterwards the rule should be strictly enforced to the very letter of the law.

Thru 1879 – 9 balls needed for a walk

1880 – 8 balls

1881 – 7 balls

1884 – 6 balls

1886 – 7 balls

1887 – 5 balls

1889 – 4 balls

7 - Balks

1873 Rule - Whenever the player delivering the ball to the bat shall throw it by an overhand or round arm throw, the umpire shall declare a foul balk, and should the player delivering such balls to the bat persist in his action, the umpire, after warning him of the penalty, shall declare the game forfeited by a score of 9 to 0. Also, when the player delivering the ball makes any motion to deliver the ball to the bat, he shall so deliver it, and he must not have either foot outside the lines of his position, either when commencing to deliver the ball or at the time of its delivery; and if he fail in any of these particulars, then it shall be declared a balk, in which case any base runner occupying a base shall take one base without being put out.

1900 – Rule 32. — Balking.

A Balk shall be :

Section I. Any motion made by the pitcher to deliver the ball to the bat or to first base without delivering it.

Sic. 2. The throwing of the ball by the pitcher to any base to catch the base-runner without first stepping directly towards said base immediately before throwing the ball.

Sec. 3. Any delivery of the ball to the bat by the pitcher while his (pivot) foot is not in contact with the pitcher's plate, and he is not facing the batsman, as defined in Rule 29.

Sec. 4. Any motion in delivering the ball to the bat by the pitcher while not in the position defined in Rule 29.

SEC. 5. The holding of the ball by the pitcher so long as, in the opinion of the umpire, to delay the game unnecessarily.

SBC. 6. Standing in position and making any motion to pitch without having the ball in his possession.

SEC. 7. The making of any motion the pitcher habitually makes in his method of delivery, without his immediately delivering the ball to the bat.

SEC 8. If the pitcher delivers the ball to the bat when the catcher is standing outside the lines of the catcher's position as defined in Rule 3.

If the pitcher fails to comply with the requirements of any section of this rule the umpire must call " A balk."

By 1934 there were 13 different ways a Pitcher could balk. That has stayed to the present day in 2025

PENALTY OR PLAY OPTION

1954 - 8.05 on the penalty for a balk being runner(s) advancing a base, added, "unless the batter hits the pitch on which the balk is made, in which case the manager of the offensive team may elect to accept either the balk penalty of the results of the batter's action."

Gone in a year

1955 – 8.05 was changed to have a play override a balk if all runners, including the batter-runner, advance at least one base. It contained no provision for the manager having a choice of accepting the play or the balk

2025

Balks - If there is a runner, or runners, it is a balk when:

(1)   The pitcher, while touching his plate, makes any motion naturally associated with his pitch and fails to make such delivery;

(2) The pitcher, while touching his plate, feints a throw to first or third base and fails to complete the throw;

(3)   The pitcher, while touching his plate, fails to step directly toward a base before throwing to that base;

(4) The pitcher, while touching his plate, throws, or feints a throw to an unoccupied base, except for the purpose of making a play;

(5) The pitcher makes an illegal pitch;(quick pitch)

(6) The pitcher delivers the ball to the batter while he is not facing the batter;

(7) The   pitcher makes any motion naturally associated with his pitch while he is not touching the pitcher's plate;

(8) The pitcher unnecessarily delays the game;

(9)   The pitcher, without having the ball, stands on or astride the pitcher's plate or while off the plate, he feints a

pitch;

(10)   The pitcher, after coming to a legal pitching position, removes one hand from the ball other than in an actual pitch, or in throwing to a base;

(11)   The pitcher, while touching his plate, accidentally or intentionally has the ball slip or fall out of his hand or glove;

(12)   The pitcher, while giving an intentional base on balls, pitches when the catcher is not in the catcher's box;

(13)   The pitcher delivers the pitch from Set Position without coming to a stop.

7th inning - Substitutes

Holy Cow! – Substitutes

In the beginning substitutes were not allowed unless a player was injured during the game and was unable to continue playing. Then when substitution was allowed it got out of hand when a player already in the lineup could pinch run for another active player.. They got it right eventually but not until 1951.

In the early days they weren't big on substitutions. The starters were expected to finish the game. They did, however have to have an allowance for injuries. An interesting fact about base running subs was that the opposing Captain would pick the pinch base runner. Yes, the opposing Captain. You know he is going to pick the slowest man for the job.

1 - Substitute rules

1873 - No player shall be allowed a substitute in running the bases, except for illness or injury, unless by a special consent of the captain of the opposing nine; and in such case the latter shall select the player to run as substitute

55

1877 - Rule 2, section 3 – substitutes in general

No player shall be replaced by another player after the commencement of the second inning except for reason of illness or injury.

Rule 6, section 14 – base running substitutes.

No player shall be allowed a substitute in running the bases except for illness or injury. In such cases the **opposing Captain** shall select the man to run as substitute

1889 substitutes allowed

Rule 28, Sections 1-3: (1) In every championship game each team shall be required to have present on the field, in uniform, at least one or more substitute players. (2) One player, whose name shall be printed on the scorecard as an extra player, may be substituted at the end of any completed innings by either club, but the player retired shall not thereafter participate in the game. In addition thereto a substitute may be allowed at any time in place of a player disabled in the game then being played by reason of illness or injury, of the nature and extent of which the Umpire shall be the sole judge. (3) The Base Runner shall not have a substitute run for him, except by consent of the Captains of the contesting teams. [Section 3 restored the opportunity for a substitute runner with consent of the opposing team; since 1881 in the National League, the rule prohibited a substitute for a runner regardless of consent of the other team.]

(This is a very important rule, and the changes introduced require to be well understood. Under this rule as it now is the Captain of either nine is given the power to introduce three distinct pitchers in the game, viz., the one originally named in the batting order, and two extra men. Or he can change his battery entire by substituting a pitcher and catcher. This too, is independent of any substitution of players for those who may be disabled by illness or injury. These changes of players in putting in extra men, too, can be made at any period of innings or of a game.)

Section 3 remained the same, but this was added in parentheses: (A substitute for a Base Runner – and he only – can be introduced by consent of the opposing nine's Captain. If he refuses, that ends it. He can of course, designate the particular substitute he allows to run.)

In 1934 they had an interesting rule that allowed a player in the line up to run for another player in the line up.

1934 - Rule 17, Section 3 - A base runner shall not have a player whose name appears in the batting order of his team run for him except by consent of the Manager or Captain of the other team

1946 – Player in lineup can be a substitute runner for another player in the lineup but only with the opposing teams consent.

1951 - Rule 3.05 Substitutes
Player in lineup CANNOT become a substitute runner.

2 - Substitutes and fines

Holy Cow! – Substitutes and Umpires.
Around 1910 the substitution rules stated that a team's Captain must inform the Umpire when a substitute came into the game. If the Captain failed to do so the Umpire could fine the Captain $25. Furthermore the Umpire was required to announce the substitution to the spectators or

he would be fined $25 by the baseball Commissioner. That rule was still in effect as late as 1951.

1934 - Rule 17, section 6   - <u>Fines for not informing of substitution</u>

The Umpire can fine the Manager or Captain $25 if they fail to inform him of a substitution. The league President can fine the Umpire $25 if he fails to inform the spectators of a substitution.

Rule 60, section 2 - <u>Fined for not informing of substitution</u>

Umpire can still fine the Manager or Captain $25 if not informed of a substitution.

1946 – substitute rule $25 fine remains per 1946 rule book

1951 - League President can fine Manager or Captain for failing to announce a substitute. Not to exceed $25.

1970 - No mention about fines if substitutes not announced (changed sometime between 1951 and 1970)

8th inning – offbeat rules

Some offbeat but rules of interest

Running in reverse

Holy Cow! – You cannot run the bases in reverse.
Rule 52 in 1920 outlawed running the bases in reverse
order for the purpose of making a travesty of the game.
This one was still in the rules in 2012

Flying starts

Holy Cow! – Flying starts.
A 1954 rule put an end to flying starts. Before that a
runner on 3rd base could back up a few steps when a fly
ball was hit to the outfield in order to get a running start
when tagging up,

Position player pitching

2025 – rule 4.03 (c)(4) – no player on the lineup card other
than those designates as two-way players or pitchers may
appear as a pitcher except

(A) Following the ninth inning of an extra game.

(B) In any game in which his team is losing by at least 8 runs.

(C) Any game in which his team is winning by at least 10 runs in the ninth inning

Penalty or play

1954 - 8.05 on the penalty for a balk being runner(s) advancing a base, added, "unless the batter hits the pitch on which the balk is made, in which case the manager of the offensive team may elect to accept either the balk penalty of the results of the batter's action."

1955 also penalty or play

8.05 was changed to have a play override a balk if all runners, including the batter-runner, advance at least one base. It contained no provision for the manager having a choice of accepting the play or the balk.

Holy Cow! – Penalty or play.
Such options are common in football but they also exist in baseball and have been around for some 60 years. It happens in both Catcher's interference and Pitcher's balk situations. Originally a batter was awarded first base if a

Catcher interfered with his swing, but in 1964 the rule was modified if the batter hit the pitch while being interfered with. In such cases the offensive team manager had the choice of taking the free base penalty or the result of the play if the batted ball was more favorable. (like a home run maybe)

7 inning games

Holy Cow! – 7 inning games
Rule books in the 1950's had the provision for allowing the second game of a doubleheader to last just 7 innings. It was seldom, if ever observed and the rule disappeared when twin bills became rare, until the Covid year of 2020 when both games of doubleheaders were 7 innings

1951 Rule 4.12 (a) - second game of a doubleheader may be 7 innings.

1957 - 4.10(a) – Note added: A league may adopt a rule providing that one game of a double-header shall be seven innings in length

Benefit of the doubt

Holy Cow! – Benefit of the doubt.
This goes all the way back to 1877 and can still be found in the 1950 rule book. Simply put, if a hard hit ball that results in the batter being safe at first base, rule it a hit rather than an error. Later official scorers still go by that principle.

1877 – On a sharp hit ball, score a hit and exempt the fielder from an error
1950 – Always give the batter the benefit of the doubt and score a hit when exceptionally good fielding fails to result in an out.

Slow handling

Holy Cow! – Slow handling.
The 1955 rule 10.11 says "slow handling of the ball which does not involve mechanical misplay should not be considered an error. Huh! What does mechanical misplay mean?

1955 – Slow handling of a ball should not be considered an error.

Mental mistakes

Holy Cow! – Mental mistakes.
The 1967 rule 10.13 states that mental mistakes or misjudgments are not to be scored as errors unless specifically covered in the rules. Huh?

1967 – Mental mistakes and misjudgments are not to be scored as errors

The jewelry rule

Holy Cow! – The Jewelry rule
With the modern player's tendency to wear jewelry while playing, it's not surprising that the topic eventually appeared in the official rules. In 2019 the rule regarding hit by a pitch stated that a pitched ball hitting a batter's jewelry (necklace, bracelet, etc,) would NOT constitute a Hit by Pitch.

Still in effect in 2025

9th inning - rules are made to be broken

A quick look at some of the rules that have been ignored

1 - Fraternization

1951 - Rule 3.11 – Players cannot fraternize with opposing players while in uniform

1965 Rule 3.09 - Players of opposing teams shall not fraternize while in uniform.

2025 – Rule 4.06 - Players in uniform shall not address or mingle with spectators, nor sit in the stands before, during, or after a game. No manager, coach or player shall address any spectator before or during a game. Players of opposing teams shall not fraternize at any time while in uniform

2 - Coach's box

1877 Rule – The Captain and one assistant can coach base runners but must not approach within 15 feet of the foil line.

1905 Rule - The coacher shall be restricted to coaching the base runner only, and shall not address remarks expect to the base runner, and then only in words of assistance and direction in running bases. He shall not, by words or signs, incite or try to incite the spectators to demonstrations, and shall not use language which will in any manner refer to or reflect upon a player of the opposite club, the umpire or the spectators, Not more than two coachers, who must be players in the Uniform of the team at bat, shall be allowed to occupy the space between the players' and the coachers' lines, one near first and the other near third base, to coach base runners. If there be more than the legal number of coachers or this rule be violated in any respect the captain of the opposite side may call the attention of the umpire to the offense, and thereupon the umpire must order the illegal coacher or coachers to the bench, and if his order be not obeyed within one minute, the umpire shall assess a fine of $5.00 against each offending player, and upon a repetition of die offense, the offending player or players shall he debarred from further participation in the game, and shall have the playing field forthwith.

1951 - Rule 4.05 – Coaches must remain in the coaches box at all times

Revised Comment to require a coach, until a batted ball passes him, to position himself no closer to home plate than the front edge of the coach's box and no closer to fair territory than the side edge of the coach's box. (Rule 4.05)

1965 Rule 4.05 - Base Coaches shall remain in coach's box at all times.

2025 – Rule 5.03 (c) Base coaches must remain within the coach's box consistent with this Rule, except that a coach who has a play at his base may leave the coach's box to signal the player to slide, advance or return to a base if the coach does not interfere with the play in any manner. Other than exchanging equipment, all base coaches shall refrain from physically touching base runners, especially when signs are being given

3 - Equipment on field

Rule not enforced, stuff always left in on deck circle

1951 - Rule 3.14 - Fielders can no longer leave gloves on the field.

No equipment should be left on the field, in fair or foul grounds

1954 - 3.16 added, "Members of the offensive team shall carry all gloves and other equipment off the field and to the dugout while their team is at bat. No equipment shall be left lying on the field, either in fair or foul territory."

1965 Rule 3.14 - Members of offensive team shall carry all gloves and other equipment off the field and to the dugout when their team is at bat.

1970 Rule 3.14 - Players must take gloves to the dugout when their team is coming to bat. No equipment shall be left lying on the field, in fair or foul territory

2025 – Rule 3.10 (a)   Members of the offensive team shall carry all gloves and other equipment off the field and to the dugout while their team is at bat. No equipment shall be left lying on the field, either in fair or foul territory.

4 - Colored bats and gloves

1946 Rule 21 – the Pitcher's glove must be uniform in color

1989 Rule 1.10 D – no colored bats allowed

2006 - 1.15(a) and 1.15(c) amended rules on pitchers wearing multi-colored gloves. (a) added that the glove cannot be, n the judgment of the umpire, "distracting in any manner." (c) was added for the umpire-in-chief to remove a glove from the game if it violates the rules.

2025 - Rule 3.02(d) No colored bat may be used in a professional game unless approved by Major League Baseball

5 - Commercialization

1988 Rules - <u>uniforms</u>
Rule 1.11 (a) - all uniforms for a team must be identical

Rule 1,11 (h) – no commercialization allowed on uniforms

2025 Rules - Rule 3.03

(a)All players shall wear uniforms identical in color and style

(b)Commercialization on uniforms is allowed if approved by the Baseball Commissioner

2025 - Rule 3.03(j)   No part of the uniform shall include patches or designs relating to commercial advertisements. Notwithstanding the foregoing or anything else in these Rules, a Club may license to third- party commercial sponsors the right to place their name, logos and/or marks on the uniform, provided that the patch or design is approved in advance by the Office of the Commissioner after consultation with the Players Association.

2025 Rule 3.09 Undue Commercialization

Playing equipment including but not limited to the bases, pitcher's plate, baseball, bats, uniforms, catcher's mitts, first baseman's gloves, infielders' and outfielders' gloves and protective helmets, as detailed in the provisions of this rule, shall not contain any undue commercialization of the product. Designations by the manufacturer on any such equipment must be in good taste as to the size and content of the manufacturer's logo or the brand name of the item. The provisions of this Rule 3.09 shall apply

6 - Batter's box

2025 Rule 5.04

Batter's box – there are 9 cases when a batter may leave the box

(A) The batter shall keep at least one foot in the batter's box throughout the batter's time at bat, unless one of the following exceptions applies, in which case the batter may leave the batter's box but not the dirt area surrounding home plate:

(i)The batter swings at a pitch;

(ii) An attempted check swing is appealed to a base umpire;

(iii) The batter is forced off balance or out of the batter's box by a pitch;

(iv) A member of either team requests and is granted "Time";

(v)A defensive player attempts a play on a runner at any base;

(vi)The batter feints a bunt;

(vii)A wild pitch or passed ball occurs;

(viii) The pitcher leaves the dirt area of the pitching mound after receiving the ball;

 (ix) The catcher leaves the catcher's box to give defensive signals.

If the batter intentionally leaves the batter's box and delays play, and none of the exceptions listed in Rule 5.04(b)(4)(A)(i) through (ix) applies, the umpire shall issue a warning to the batter for the batter's first violation of this Rule in a game. For a batter's second or subsequent violations of this Rule in a game, the Office of the Commissioner may issue an appropriate discipline.

Postgame – History of rule changes

Yearly changers of baseball rules

1845 - The first important set of written rules was scribed by Alexander Cartwright, of the Knickerbocker Base Ball Club, and published on September 20, 1845. These 20 rules became known as the "Knickerbocker Rules." The "original 20 rules of baseball" were not very specific and only 14 actually were rules pertaining to the field and the play. One significant rule, Rule 13, stated that a player could not be put out by being hit by a thrown ball

1845 - fair and foul balls caught on 1 bounce were an out

1845 - 3 swings and misses are an out

1845 - balk is indicated but not defined

1845 - game ends at 21 runs

1854 - Prior to the famous Base Ball Convention in 1857 was a meeting that occurred between three New York teams on April 1, 1854, in New York City. The teams in attendance were Knickerbocker, Gotham and the Eagle clubs and they revised the "original 20 Rules." One important addition was rule 13 which stated that the first "striker" or batter of the following inning would be the batter who proceeds the player who made the third "hand," or out

1857 - Adams changed the length of the game to nine equal innings, instead of declaring the first team to score 21 "aces" or runs, the winner. Adams also declared that five innings must be played to be declared a game.

He set the distance between bases at 30 yards. It has been assumed that the distance was 30 paces between all bases although this distance was never specified in the original Knickerbocker Rules. The only mention of distance is listed in Rule 4 and states; "The bases shall be from "home" to second base, 42 paces; from first to third base, 42 paces, equidistant."

The pitching distance was also not described in the Knickerbocker Rules. Adams set the distance from the 12' pitcher's line (which is centered to an imaginary line that is between home base and second base and extends from third to first) to home base at 45 feet.

It was agreed upon that if the striker swung and missed at three pitched balls and the third pitched ball was caught on the first bound or on the fly, the batter was out. If it was not caught on the first bound or the fly the batter must attempt to "make his first," or run to first.

No ace or base could be made upon a foul ball, or when a fair ball has been caught without having touched the ground; and the ball shall, in both instances, be considered dead and not in play, until it shall first have been settled in the hands of the pitcher. When a fair ball has been caught without having touched the ground, the players running the bases shall have the privilege of returning to them.

1857 - 9 players on a team
1857 - balk is defined as 2 feet behind line and ball cannot be jerked or thrown, just pitched
1857- called strikes after warning
1857 - game is 9 innings
1857 - pitcher can pitch at any speed and may apply spin to the ball

1858 - For the first time the umpire is allowed to call strikes on a batter that repeatedly refuses not swing at good balls. The umpire was required to warn the striker before calling a strike. After three strikes were called, the batter was bound to "make his run" to first base if the last called strike was not caught by the catcher on the fly or first bound

1858 - a batter was out if a ball, fair or foul, was caught on the fly or after one bounce.

1859 - The bat is limited to 2 and 1/2 inches in diameter (before this a bat like that used in cricket with a 4-inch-wide flat face had been commonplace).

1860 - The umpire of a game is selected by the captain of each team. He is given the authority to suspend play, and he must make a call when a ball is foul

1860 - The striker is required to stand on a line that extends three feet on either side of home base and is parallel to the pitcher's line.

1860 - The umpire was instructed to warn a batter, before calling strikes, if he repeatedly did not strike at fair pitched balls. After three called strikes and the last strike caught on the first bound or the fly the batter was out. If the ball was not caught on the first bound or the fly the batter had to make his first.

1862 - – called balls and bases on balls introduced (9 balls)

1862 - Pitchers box was 12 feet by 3 feet and a year later it became 12 X 4 feet but the pitcher could not move around. He could not take a step with his delivery and had to pitch with both feet on the ground

1863 - The umpires are allowed to call unfair pitched balls. After a warning is given the batter takes his base after three called balls.

1863 - All base runners advance one base, regardless of being forced or not, when the batter receives his base on called balls.

1863 - The pitcher is not permitted to take even a step in his delivery. Both feet must be on the ground when he releases the ball.

1863 - The bat must be round and of wood. Its width is still limited to 2 1/2 inches, but its length is not restricted

1864 - When a runner circles the bases, he must touch each one

1864 - batter calls for high or low pitch

1864 - called balls and bases on balls (but not all pitches have to be called

1864 - pitcher had to pitch with both feet on the ground

1864 - pitchers box eliminated running starts

1864 - pitchers box moved from 45 to 50 feet

1865 - The pitcher's box "twelve feet by three feet" replaces the twelve-foot line.

1865 - Fair hit balls must be caught on the fly. Foul balls may still be caught on the fly or the first bound

1866 - The pitcher's box is enlarged to a four by twelve foot rectangle

1866 - pitchers box narrowed to 6 feet wide

1866 - no more one bounce outs on fair balls (still ok for fouls until 1883)

1867 - the batter was given the right to call for a high or low pitch.

1867 - The pitcher's box is six feet by six feet.

1867 - Pitchers are allowed to take as many steps as they like in their delivery

1867 - Pitcher is allowed to move around in his box

1867 - The batter is not allowed to step forward or backward when striking at the ball.

1868 - The pitcher's box shrinks to a four by six foot box.

1868 - The bat is to be no more than forty-two inches long.

1868 - The batter is allowed to only step forward when striking at the ball

1868 - pitcher can lift foot when delivering a pitch

1868 - the pitchers box is now 6 feet by 6 feet

1869 - The pitcher's box is a six-foot square

1869 - After the striker receives his base on called balls, only base runners that are forced to, move one base

1870 - The first pitched ball is not to be called

1871 - The National Association of Base-Ball Players begins play and is the first professional baseball league in the United States. The last year of operation would be 1875.

1871 - The striker may call for a low or high pitched ball. A "low ball" is ball that is a fair ball that is between the knees and the waist of the striker. A "high ball" is a ball that is a fair ball that is between the striker's waist and shoulders.

1871 - The striker is permitted to overrun first base provided that he returns without attempting to run to second.

1872 - "Unfair" balls are identified as any ball that is delivered over the striker's head, hit the ground in front of home base, delivered to the opposite side that the batter strikes from or come within one foot of the batter. These types of pitches are required to be called in the order they are delivered after the first ball is pitched

1872 - Pitchers wrist snap legalized (common use but seldom enforced though illegal)

1876 - The National League becomes the second professional baseball league in the United States. It is still in existence today.

1876 - The umpire was allowed, during the game, to ask a bystander whether a catch had been fairly made before rendering a decision.

1876 - If an umpire is unable to see whether a catch has been fairly made, he may confer with spectators and players.

1876 – Rule 5, Section 5. The bat must be round, and must not exceed two and one-half inches in

diameter in the thickest part. It must be wholly of wood, and shall not exceed forty-two inches in length

1877 - To choose an umpire the league selects "three gentlemen of repute" in each city where there is a team. At least three hours before a game the <u>visiting team</u> chooses the umpire from among them.

1877 - A time at bat is not charged to a batter who walks.

1877 - Canvas-covered bases are required. They are fifteen inches square, the same as today.

1877 - Home plate is relocated to its present spot

1877 - If a batted ball strikes a base runner, while not occupying a base, he is declared out

1879 - walk is 7 balls

1879 – Pitcher had to face batter before pitching to him

1879 - 3 strikes were an out

1879 - An umpire's fees and expenses are paid by the visiting club.

1879 - An umpire is given the power to impose fines of not less than ten dollars and not more than twenty dollars when he thinks it's necessary.

1879 - All pitched balls must be called strikes, balls, or fouls.

1879 - There are nine balls in a walk.

1880 - The runner hit by a batted ball is out.

1880 - The base on balls decreases to eight.

1880 - The limits of the fines an umpire may impose change. Now it's not less than five dollars and not more than fifty dollars.

1880 – front of pitchers box was 50 feet from the center of home plate

1880 - Pitchers were allowed to throw sidearm

1880 - a batter was out if the catcher caught the third strike; otherwise the batter got four strikes.

1881 - The base on balls is seven.

1881 - The pitching distance is lengthened to fifty feet.

1881 - The pitcher is fined for deliberately hitting a batter with the ball.

1881 - A spectator who "hisses or hoots" at or insults the umpire may be ejected from the grounds.

1881 - The base runner may no longer be put out when he is returning to his base on a foul ball.

1882 - The three-foot base line is adopted.

1882 - Umpires may not reverse decisions on matters of judgment.

1882 - Umpires may not confer with spectators or players.

1882 - The American League is formed.

1882 – Pitchers can now throw ball from above the waist

1882 - The American Association is formed. It would operate until 1891 and then be absorbed and combined with the National League.

1883 - A foul ball caught on the bounce ceases to be an out. It must be caught before it touches the ground.

1883 - An error is charged to the pitcher for a base on balls, wild pitch, hit batter, and balk.

1883 - Pitching is allowed from anywhere up to shoulder height

1883 - Pitcher can throw shoulder high deliveries

1883 - Walk is 6 balls

1884 - Almost all restrictions on a pitcher's motion are lifted. He may throw the ball with virtually any motion he chooses, provided that his delivery is not higher than his shoulders and he is facing the batter at the moment of wind-up. He is allowed only one step before delivery.

1884 - The pitcher is allowed to deliver the ball to the batter in any manner

1884   pitchers can throw overhand

1884 - A base on balls is six.

1885 - Home base may be made of marble or whitened rubber.

1885 - The pitcher is credited with an assist on a strike-out.

1885 - One side of the bat could be flat (until 1893)

1886 - A base on balls is five.

1886 - The pitcher's box becomes four feet by seven feet.

1886 - An umpire may introduce a new ball at any time. Before this year, when a ball was lost, the umpire gave the team five minutes to find it before he threw in a new one. An umpire must have two baseballs at his disposal at all times.

1886 - First and third base are moved within the foul lines.

1886 - A hit batsman is not charged with a time at bat.

1886 - No stolen base is credited to a runner for bases advanced by his own volition.

1886 – Calling for high or low pitches abolished

1886 - 5 balls became a walk

1887 - The pitcher's box is 4 feet by 5 1/2 feet.

1887 - A pitcher must keep one foot on the rear line of the box and may not take more than one step in delivering the ball. Before delivery, he must hold the ball in front of him so that it is visible to the umpire.

1887 - No error is charged to the pitcher for a base on balls, wild pitch, hit batter, and balk.

1887 - The umpire may call a game if the spectators are disorderly. The maximum fine for arguing with an ump or protesting a call is ten dollars.

1887 - The batter is no longer allowed to request a high or low pitch.

1887 - A strike-out is called on four strikes. (This rule lasted only one season.)

1887 - Home plate is to be made of rubber and is to be twelve inches square.

1887 - A base on balls is scored as a hit and counted as a time at bat. This rule lasted one season only.

1887 - A strike was defined as a fair ball that was between the batter's knees and shoulders.

1887 - The batsman was awarded first base after being hit by a pitched ball only if he attempted to avoid the ball.

1887 - Batter can no longer call for location of pitch

1887 - Strike zone defined as shoulders to the knees

1887 - Walks count as hits for that year only

1887 - Warning strike eliminated, 4 strikes were a strikeout just that year

1887 - The rules were changed so that batters could no longer call for a pitch;

1888 - A base on balls is not counted as a hit and not charged as a time at bat.

1888 - If a runner is hit by a batted ball, the batter is credited with a hit.

1888 - The strikeout is back to three strikes.

1888 - It is a ground-rule double instead of a home run if the ball is batted over the fence in fair territory where the fence is less than 210 feet from home plate.

1888 - The mandatory fine for a coach who leaves the coach's box to protest a call is $5.

1888 - An error is charged to the pitcher for a base on balls, wild pitch, hit batter, and balk.

1888 - A hit batsman is awarded first base and credited with a hit.

1888 - A batter is credited with a hit when his batted ball hits a base runner.

1889 - No error is charged to the pitcher for a base on balls, wild pitch, hit batter, and balk. A pitcher is not credited with an assist on a strikeout.

1889 - The sacrifice bunt is statistically recognized, but the batter is charged with a time at bat.

1889 - 4 balls are a walk,

1889 - 3 strikes are an out

1889 - Any fair batted ball that was hit over a fence less than 210 feet from home plate entitled the Batsman to two bases.

1890 - The Players' National League of Base Ball Clubs is formed and plays its only season. It becomes the first league to institute what is now known as "the infield fly rule." The rule stated that if a Base Runner was on first base and there were less than two outs and the Batsman made a fair hit so that the ball would fall within the infield and the ball touches any fielder whether held by him or not before it touches the ground, the Batsman was out.

1891 - Pitchers box eliminated and replaced by a rubber slab 12 inches by 4 inches.

1891 - Pitcher must keep rear foot on slab

1891 - Substitutions are allowed at any time during a game, but once he has been substituted for, a player may not return.

1892 - It's a ground-rule double instead of a home run if the ball is hit over the fence in fair territory if the fence is less than 235 feet from home plate.

1892 - Bats were no longer allowed a flat side and had to be round.

1892 - The 154 game schedule was adopted.

1893 – Pitcher's slab moved from 50 feet and center of plate to 60 feet 6 inches to rear of home plate

1893 - Flat bats no longer allowed

1893 - A batter credited with a sacrifice is not charged with a time at bat.

1893 - The pitcher's box disappears (never to be seen again) and is replaced by the rubber slab twelve inches long and four inches wide.

1893 - The pitcher is required to place his rear foot against the slab.

1893 - The NLAABBC's first attempt at the modern day infield fly rule is instituted. It stated that the batter is out if a fly ball is hit that can be handled by an infielder with first base occupied with only one out.

1894 - The batter is out if, with two strikes, a bunt attempt results in a foul hit.

1894 - Foul bunts were made strikes, and the infield fly rule was adopted with one out.

1895 - The pitcher's rubber is enlarged to its present size of 24 by 6 inches.

1895 - The maximum diameter of the bat is increased to 2 3/4 inches, where it remains today.

1895 - The infield fly rule is adopted: the umpire may call an infield fly when there is one out and first and second or first, second, and third base are occupied.

1895 - A strike is charged to a batter for a foul tip.

1895 - The limits on fines change again to not less than $25 and not more than $100.

1895 - If the crowd becomes so unruly that the game is stopped for more than fifteen minutes, the umpire may declare a forfeit. (If that happens, the visitors win, 9-0.)

1895 - The infield fly rule is modified. It now states that the batter is out if a fly ball is hit that can be handled by an infielder with first and second bases occupied, or first, second and third bases occupied with only one out.

1895 - A ball tipped, or a foul tip, by the Batsman which rises above his head that is caught by the catcher within the catcher's 10-foot lines, is a strike.

1896 - A $25 fine is imposed on a coach or a player who uses vulgar language. It costs players $5 to $10 for any other first offense, $25 and possibly ejection for a second offense, and mandatory ejection for a third offense

1897 - Intentionally discoloring or injuring the ball is punishable by a $5 fine. The ball is replaced

1898 - A stolen base is credited to the base runner when he reaches a base he attempts to steal without the aid of batting or fielding errors or a hit by the batter.
1898 - The first official balk rule: a pitcher is compelled to throw to a base if he makes a motion in that
1898 - The modern rule for recognizing stolen bases was adopted.

1899 - If the catcher interferes with the Batsman and prevents him from hitting the ball the Batsman is awarded first base.
1899 - The balk rule is refined: a pickoff throw may not be faked; a pitcher must complete his motion.

1900 – Home plate changed from square to 5 sided figure

1901 - Fouls not caught are strikes unless there are two strikes already

1901 - The infield fly rule was extended to apply when there were no outs.

1901 – 1902 - The first two fouls are termed strikes (in the National League).

1901 – 1902 - The catcher is no longer allowed to catch two strikes on a bounce.

1901 – 1902 - The infield fly rule is in effect when there are no outs as well as one out.

1901 – 1902 - The American League joins the majors (the National League got started in 1876), and the rule discrepancies begin. For instance, the National League declares that any foul ball not caught on the fly is a strike unless the batter has two strikes on him. The AL does not agree at least not right away.

1901 – 1902 - If an offense is "flagrant" enough, the league president may suspend a player or coach who has been fined and/or ejected by an umpire.

1903 - If there is only one umpire in a game, he may stand anywhere on the field he likes.

1903 - The American League agrees that any foul ball not

caught on the fly is a strike unless the batter has two strikes on him.

1907 - The sacrifice fly rule was adopted.

1908 - Pitchers are forbidden to scuff or soil a new ball.
1908 - The sacrifice fly rule is adopted, exempting the batter from an at-bat when a run scores after a catch.

1909 - The pitcher or catcher is charged with an error if a batter reaches first base on a wild pitch or passed ball.
1909 - A bunt on a third strike is a strikeout. The catcher is credited with the putout.
1909 - If a runner is thrown out on an attempted double-steal, neither runner shall be credited with a stolen base.

1910 - Cork centers were added to balls.

1910 – 1911 The captain of a team must notify the umpire-in-chief of any substitution.
1910 – 1911 An umpire must warn players on the bench for excessive yelling before he can fine or otherwise punish them for it.

1912 – 1913 - Earned runs are charged to a pitcher when a player scores by means of safe hits, sacrifice hits, bases on balls, hit batters, wild pitches, and balks

1914 – 1916 - In the case of fire, panic, or storm, the umpire does not have to wait until the pitcher has the ball on the mound to call a time-out.

1917 – Freak deliveries including the SPITBALL were outlawed
1917 - Balk if catcher is not in his box when pitcher releases the ball

1917 – 1919 - Earned runs are also charged to a pitcher when a player scores by means of a stolen base

1920 - The abolition of the spitball, with a "grandfather clause": each team is allowed to appoint two spitball pitchers for the 1920 season.
1920 - A ball that hits an umpire is in play.
1920 - The umpire may suspend play at any time for an accident with a player or an umpire.

1920 - After a thirty-minute rain delay, an umpire may terminate a game.

1920 - The category of RBI is added to scoring.

1920 - A runner may not run the bases in reverse order "for the purpose of confusing the fielders or making a travesty of the game."

1920 - The ball has its gloss removed before a game by the umpire.

1920 - Enter the "lively ball." Australian yarn, said to be stronger than its American equivalent, may be wound tighter, so the ball's bounce and hardness increase.

1920 - No stolen base is to be credited when the defense makes no attempt to get the runner out.

1925 - Pitchers are allowed to use a rosin bag

1925 - The minimum distance for a home run was made 250 feet.

1926 – Pitcher allowed to use a rosin bag

1926 – 1930 - Pitchers are not credited with a strikeout if a batter reaches first base because of a wild pitch on the third strike.

1926 – 1930 - It is a ground-rule double instead of a home run if the ball is hit over the fence in fair territory if the fence is less than 250 feet from home plate.

1926 – 1930 - The cushioned cork-center baseball is introduced.

1926 – 1930 - The sacrifice fly rule is amended to exempt a batter from an at-bat when a runner advances from first to second or second to third as well as on scoring.

1931 – mound must be 15 inches high

1931 – 1932 - A fair ball that bounces through or over a fence or into the stands is considered a ground-rule double instead of a home run.

1931 – 1932 - The sacrifice fly is eliminated

1939 - The pitcher is allowed to have his free foot in front of or behind the rubber, with his pivot foot in front of or on the rubber (but always in contact with it).

1939 - A batter is credited with a sacrifice fly and not charged with a time at bat if he hits a fly ball that is caught and a runner scores on the catch. This rule lasted only a year.

1940 – 1944 - A batter is no longer credited with a sacrifice fly.

1940 – 1944 - The pitcher is permitted to take two steps one forward, one backward as long as his pivot foot remains in contact with the rubber at all times.

1940 – 1944 - It is a balk if a pitcher throws or fakes a throw to an unoccupied base.

1940 – 1944 - The umpire assumes authority over trainers.

1950 - An umpire may no longer levy fines. That job is reserved for the league president.

1950 - The pitcher's mound must be fifteen inches above the level of the base lines.

1950 – Strike Zone became armpits to top of knees

1954 - A batter is credited with a sacrifice fly and not charged with a time at bat if he hits a fly ball and the runner scores on the catch.

1954 - Offensive players are required to "carry all gloves and other equipment off the field . . . while their team is at bat."

1954 - The bat may be made of two or more pieces of wood laminated together

1955 - When a base is occupied, a pitcher must deliver the pitch within twenty seconds of receiving it from the catcher. If he fails to do so, the umpire may call a ball

1956 - A base runner who interferes with a batted ball in order to break up a double play is to be declared out, as is the batter.

1961 - The 162-game schedule was adopted.

1962 – 1966 - Oversized gloves are banned for use by pitchers, infielders, and outfielders.
1962 – 1966 - Batters may apply a grip-improving substance to the bat, though not beyond eighteen inches of its length beginning at the handle.

1963 – Strike Zone enlarged – top of shoulder to top of knees

1968 - The pitcher's mound is lowered to ten inches above home plate and the base lines, where it remains today.
1968 - If a pitcher "goes to his mouth" with men on base, a balk is declared. If the bases are empty, a ball is called.

1969 - The strike zone reduced: from the armpits to the top of the knees.
1969 – 1970 - The category of Saves is added to baseball statistics.

1973 – The designated hitter in the American league (2020 in NL)

1974 - The save rule is amended slightly; no save is to be credited to a pitcher unless the tying run was on base or at the plate or unless he pitched three effective innings. (Before this a reliever was given a save if he maintained the lead, no matter what the score when he arrived.)
1974 - Umpires may declare illegal pitches without any physical evidence. If they think that the motion of the ball indicates that the pitcher is throwing a spitter or a defaced ball, they may issue a warning and, if it happens a second time, eject a pitcher from the game.

1975 - The ball may be covered with cowhide as well as horsehide.
1975 - Cupped bats are allowed.
1975 - The save is refined once more: if the tying run is on deck, a pitcher is credited with a save.

2023 – Bases increased in size from 15 to 18 inches
2023 - Defensive shifts banned
2023 - Pitch clocks introduced

Appendix 1– Knickerbocker Rules

Knickerbocker Rules (New York): 1845

1st.Members must strictly observe the time agreed upon for exercise, and be punctual in their attendance.

2nd.When assembled for exercise, the President, or in his absence, the Vice-President, shall appoint an Umpire, who shall keep the game in a book provided for that purpose, and note all violations of the By-Laws and Rules during the time of exercise.

3rd.The presiding officer shall designate two members as Captains, who shall retire and make the match to be played, observing at the same time that the players opposite to each other should be as nearly equal as possible; the choice of sides to be then tossed for, and the first in hand to be decided in like manner.

4th.The bases shall be from "home" to second base, forty-two paces; from first to third base, forty-two paces, equidistant.

5th.No stump match shall be played on a regular day of exercise.

6th.If there should not be a sufficient number of members of the Club present at the time agreed upon to commence exercise, gentlemen not members may be chosen in to make up the match, which shall not be broken up to take in members that may afterwards appear; but, in all cases, members shall have the preference, when present, at the making of a match.

7th.If members appear after the game is commenced, they may be chosen in if mutually agreed upon.

8th.The game to consist of twenty-one counts, or aces; but at the conclusion an equal number of hands must be played.

9th.The ball must be pitched, and not thrown, for the bat.

10th.A ball knocked out of the field, or outside the range of the first or third base, is foul.

11th.Three balls being struck at and missed and the last one caught, is a hand out; if not caught is considered fair, and the striker bound to run.

12th.If a ball be struck, or tipped, and caught, either flying or on the first bound, it is a hand out.

13th.A player running the bases shall be out, if the ball is in the hands of an adversary on the base, or the runner is touched with it before he makes his base; it being understood, however, that in no instance is a ball to be thrown at him.

14th.A player running who shall prevent an adversary from catching or getting the ball before making his base, is a hand out.

15th.Three hands out, all out.

16th.Players must take their strike in regular turn.

17th.All disputes and differences relative to the game, to be decided by the Umpire, from which there is no appeal.

18th.No ace or base can be made on a foul strike.

19th.A runner cannot be put out in making one base, when a balk is made by the pitcher.

20th.But one base allowed when a ball bounds out of the field when struck.

20 rules, with a little more than half pertaining to the actual playing of the game. But some were to pass the test of

time. There are still 3 strikes and you're out and still 3 outs and the opposition gets to bat. There are still 4 bases and foul balls, but the 21 Aces, or runs that sealed victory is long gone.

That was 1845 and it wasn't long before the National Association of Baseball Players came into being in 1857 and expanded on the initial Knickerbocker rules.

Appendix 2 – NABBP rules

National Association of (Amateur) Base Ball Players - 1857
RULES AND REGULATIONS, AS ADOPTED BY THE CONVENTION OF BASE BALL CLUBS, HELD FEBRUARY 25TH, 1857

Section 1

The ball must weigh not less than 6 nor more than 6 1/4 ounces avoirdupois; it must measure not less than 10, nor more than 10 1/4 inches in circumference;; it must be composed of india-rubber and yarn, and covered with leather. It shall be furnished by the challenging Club, and become the property of the winning Club, as a trophy of victory.

Section 2.

The bat must be round, and must not exceed 2 1/2 inches in diameter in the thickest part; it must be made of wood, and may be of any length, to suit the striker.

Section 3.

The bases must be four in number, placed at equal distances from each other, and securely fastened upon the four corners of a square whose sides are respectively thirty yards. They must be so constructed as to be distinctly seen by the umpires and referee, and must cover a space equal to one square foot of surface; the first, second and third bases shall be canvas bags, painted white, and filled with sand or saw-dust; the home base and pitcher's point to be each marked by a flat circular iron plate, painted or enamelled white.

Section 4.

The base from which the ball is struck shall be designated the home base, and must be directly opposite to the second base; the first base must always be that upon the right hand, and the third base that upon the left hand side of the striker, when occupying his position at the home base.

Section 5.

The pitcher's position shall be designated by a line four yards in length, drawn at right angles to a line from home to the second base, having its centre upon that line, at a fixed iron plate placed at a point fifteen yards distant from the home base.

Section 6.

The ball must be pitched, not jerked or thrown to the bat, and whenever the pitcher draws back his hand, with the apparent purpose or pretension to deliver the ball, he shall so deliver it. The pitcher must deliver the ball as near as possible, over the centre of the home base, and must have neither foot in advance of the line at the time of delivering the ball, and if he fails in either of these particulars, then it shall be declared a baulk.

Section 7.

When a baulk is made by the pitcher, every player running the bases is entitled to one base without being put out.

Section 8.

If the ball from a stroke of the bat is caught behind the range of home and the first base, or home and the third base, without having touched the ground, or first touches the ground behind those bases, it shall be termed foul, and must be so declared by the umpires, unasked. If the ball first touches the ground, or is caught without having touched the ground, either upon or in front of the range of those bases, it shall be considered fair.

Section 9.

A player making the home base, shall be entitled to score one run.

Section 10.

If three balls are struck at and missed, and the last one is not caught, either flying or upon the first bound, it shall be considered fair, and the striker must attempt to make his run.

Section 11.

The striker is out if a foul ball is caught, either before touching the ground or upon the first bound.

Section 12.

Or, if three balls are struck at and missed; and the last is caught either before touching the ground or upon the first bound.

Section 13.

Or, if a fair ball is struck, and the ball is caught either without having touched the ground or upon the first bound.

Section 14.

Or, if a fair ball is struck, and the ball is held by an adversary on on the first base, before the striker touches that base.

Section 15.

Or, if at any time hi is touched by the ball while in play in the hands of an adversary, without some part of his person being on a base.

Section 16.

No ace or base can be made upon a foul ball, nor when a fair ball has been caught without having touched the ground; and the ball shall, in both instances, be considered dead and not in play, until it shall first have been settled in the hands of the pitcher. When a fair ball has been caught without having touched the ground, the players running the bases shall have the privilege of returning to them.

Section 17.

Players must stand on a line drawn through the centre of the home base not exceeding in length three feet from either side thereof, and such line shall be parallel with the line occupied by the pitcher. They shall strike in regular rotation; and after the first innings is played, the turn commences with the player who stands on the list next to the one who lost the third hand.

Section 18.

Players must make their bases in the order of striking; and when a fair ball is struck, and not caught flying, nor on the first bound, the first base must be vacated, as also the second and third bases, if they are occupied at the same time. Players may be put out upon any base, under these circumstances, in the same manner as the striker when running to the first base.

Section 19.

Players running the bases must, so far as possible, keep

upon the direct line between the bases; and, should any player run three feet out of this line, for the purpose of avoiding the ball in the hands of an adversary, he shall be declared out.

Section 20.

Any player, who shall, intentionally, prevent an adversary from catching or fielding the ball, shall be declared out.

Section 21.

If a player is prevented from making a base, by the intentional obstruction of an adversary, he shall be entitled to that base, and not be put out.

Section 22.

If any adversary stops the ball with his hat or cap, or takes it from the hands of a party not engaged in the game, no player can be put out, unless the ball shall first have been settled in the hands of the pitcher.

Section 23.

If a ball, from the stroke of the bat, is held under any other circumstances than as enumerated in section 22, and without having touched the ground more than once, the striker is out.

Section 24.

If two hands are already out, no player, running home at

the time a ball is struck, can make an ace, if the striker is put out.

Section 25.

An innings must be concluded at the time the third hand is put out.

Section 26.

The game shall consist of nine innings to each side, when, should the number of runs be equal, the innings shall be continued until a majority of runs, upon an equal number of innings, shall be declared, which shall conclude the game.

Section 27.

In playing all matches, nine players from each club shall constitute a full field, and they must have been regular members of the club which they represent, for thirty days prior to the match. No change or substitution shall be made after the game has been commenced, unless for reason of illness or injury. Positions of players shall be determined by captains, previously appointed for that prupose by the respective clubs.

Section 28.

Any player holding membership in more than one club, at the same time, shall not be permitted to play in the matches of either club.

Section 29.

The umpires in all matches shall take care that the regulations respecting the ball, bats, bases, and the pitcher's position, are strictly observed; they shall be the judges of fair and unfair play, and shall determine all differences which may occur during the game; they shall take especial care to declare all foul balls and baulks immediately on their occurrence. They shall together select a referee, from whose decision-in case of a disagreement between them-there shall be no appeal.

Section 30.

No person engaged in a match, either as umpire, referee, or player, shall be either directly or indirectly interested in any bet upon the game. Neither umpire, referee nor player shall be changed during a match, unless with the consent of both parties, except for a violation of this law, and except as provided in section 27, and then the referee may dismiss any transgressor.

Section 31.

The umpires and referee in any match, shall determine when play shall be suspended; and if the game cannot be concluded, it shall be decided by the last even innings, provided five innings have been played; and the party having the greatest number of runs shall be declared the winner.

Section 32.

Clubs may adopt, such rules respecting balls knocked beyond or outside of the bounds of the field, as the circumstances of the ground may demand, and these rules shall govern all matches played upon the ground, provided that they are distinctly made known to every player and umpire, and the referee, previous to the commencement of the game.

Section 33.

No person shall be permitted to approach or to speak with the referee, umpires, or players, or in any manner to interrupt or interfere during the progress of the game, unless by the special request of the umpires or referee.

Section 34.

No person shall be permitted to act as umpire or referee in a match, unless he shall be a member of a Base Ball Club, governed by these rules.

Section 35.

Whenever a match shall have been determined upon between two clubs, play shall be called at the exact hour appointed; and should either party fail to produce their players within fifteen minutes thereafter, the party so failing shall admit a defeat.

Appendix 3 – Town ball rules

Town Ball, also known as the Massachusetts game

The Rules of the Massachusetts Game

by The Massachusetts Association of Base Ball Players
May 13, 1858

1. The Ball must weigh not less than two, nor more than two and three-quarters ounces, avoirdupois. It must measure not less than six and a half, nor more than eight and a half inches in circumference, and must be covered with leather.

2. The Bat must be round, and must not exceed two and a half inches in diameter in the thickest part. It must be made of wood, and may be of any length to suit the Striker.

3. Four Bases or Bounds shall constitute a round; the distance from each base shall be sixty feet.

4. The bases shall be wooden stakes, projecting four feet from the ground.

5. The Striker shall stand inside of a space of four feet in diameter, at equal distance between the first and fourth Bases.

6. The Thrower shall stand thirty-five feet from and on a parallel line with the Striker.

7. The Catcher shall not enter within the space occupied by the Striker, and must remain upon his feet in all cases while catching the Ball.

8. The Ball must be thrown - not pitched or tossed - to the Bat, on the side preferred by the Striker, and within reach of his Bat.

9. The ball must be caught flying in all cases.

10. Players must take their knocks in the order in which they are numbered; and after the first inning is played, the turn will commence with the player succeeding the one who lost on the previous inning.

11. The Ball being struck at three times and missed, and caught each time by a player on the opposite side, the Striker shall be considered out. Or, if the Ball be ticked or knocked, and caught on the opposite side, the Striker shall be considered out. But if the ball is not caught after being struck at three times, it shall be considered a knock, and the Striker obliged to run.

12. Should the Striker stand at the Bat without striking at good balls thrown repeatedly at him, for the apparent purpose of delaying the game, or of giving advantage to players, the referees, after warning him, shall call one strike, and if he persists in such action, two and three strikes; when three strikes are called, he shall be subject to the same rules as if he struck at three fair balls.

13. A player, having possession of the first Base, when the Ball is struck by the succeeding player, must vacate the Base, even at the risk of being put out; and when two players get on one Base, either by accident or otherwise, the player who arrived last is entitled to the Base.

14. If a player, while running the Bases, be hit with the Ball thrown by one of the opposite side, before he has touched the home bound, while off a Base, he shall be considered out.

15. A player, after running the four Bases, on making the home bound, shall be entitled to one tally.

16. In playing all match games, when one is out, the side shall be considered out.

17. In playing all match games, one hundred tallies shall constitute the game, the making of which by either Club, that Club shall be judged the winner.

18. Not less than ten nor more than fourteen players from each Club, shall constitute a match in all games.

19. A person engaged on either side, shall not withdraw during the progress of the match, unless he be disabled, or by the consent of the opposite party.

20. The Referees shall be chosen as follows: One from each Club, who shall agree upon a third made from some Club belonging to this Association, if possible. Their decision shall be final, and binding upon both parties.

21. The Tallymen shall be chosen in the same manner as the Referees.

Printed in Dunstable, United Kingdom

THE

DAVID GILMOUR

STORY

FROM PINK FLOYD TO SOLO STARDOM AND BEYOND

BY

MARIA J. SHERMAN